JUNKYARD JEWELS
DIAMONDS IN THE RUST

PAT KYTOLA & LARRY KYTOLA

MBI Publishing Company

This book is dedicated to my husband, Larry, who did most of the photography, and my son, Brad; without their time and cooperation, this project would never have been completed.

First published in 1989 by MBI Publishing Company, Galtier Plaza, Suite 200, 380 Jackson Street, St. Paul, MN 55101-3885 USA

MBI Publishing Company books are also available at discounts in bulk quantity for industrial or sales-promotional use. For details write to Special Sales Manager at Motorbooks International Wholesalers & Distributors, Galtier Plaza, Suite 200, 380 Jackson Street, St. Paul, MN 55101-3885 USA.

Library of Congress Cataloging-in-Publication Data Available

ISBN 0-7603-1204-4

Printed in China

Special acknowledgment is due Judy Measner for her encouragement, proofreading, and input.

I would like to thank my son, Brad, for the idea for the title of this book. I would also like to acknowledge the following people and automobile owners: Ted, Randy, Jenny and Amy Jacobson; Jerry and Karol Iverson; Ken and Kathy Bird; Todd Buer family; Paul Schlstrom; Harry Johnson; Jim's Auto Salvage; Windy Hills Auto Parts; Weekly's Auto Parts; Zeigler King Salvage; Park River Auto Salvage; Jim Gruver family; Dick's Service and Salvage.

Also, the many other owners whose names remain unknown to me.

Contents

Preface

It's December in western Wisconsin. Outside my window the snow is softly falling, as if it were eiderdown. *American Graffiti* is playing on the television set, but I don't see it, only hear it, being lost in my own memories. My thoughts drift to this past summer spent traveling with my family throughout Minnesota, Wisconsin, Iowa, North and South Dakota, photographing salvage yards. We headed west through the Minneapolis-St. Paul area, across Highway 7 to Hutchinson, Minnesota, down Highway 15 into Sleepy Eye, then a jog up to Marshall and down into Sioux Falls. In South Dakota we traveled on Interstate 90 and Highway 18, then south into Iowa.

As autumn neared, we journeyed north on Highway 10 in Minnesota until we came to Highway 2, which took us into Grand Forks, North Dakota. In Wisconsin we explored the Indianhead country, north to the Great Lakes, and to Interstate 90 in the south. We didn't stay on the beaten path, but instead went out of our way to enjoy the scenery of the backroads, many of them unpaved.

It's been said that the only place left to find good tin is in the American Southwest, but as you leaf through the following pages, you may change your mind. Yes, it is true that the salt, humidity, mud, and crushers have taken their toll on the cars in the Midwest, but some still remain.

Whether you are an armchair enthusiast or an avid hunter of tin, wander with me through the pages of this book and relive an era in America's past—gone but never to be forgotten.

Go change into your old blue jeans, sweatshirt, and tennis shoes, put the fifties music on the stereo, pull up the easy chair and pretend you're cruising down the highway with me in my 1931 Model A Ford.

Let's go tin hunting.

Lush clumps of yellow wildflowers make bright spots of color alongside this lonely building. You never know where you will find tin hiding! Do you suppose that there are more hidden inside this weathered garage near Ashland, Wisconsin? An abandoned house lies just to the left of the garage, outside this picture, beside which sit two more vintage cars.

Diamonds in golden settings

Many of our memories are intertwined with the American automobile. Do you remember Pearl Harbor and the shortage of cars due to the war's appetite for metal? Do you remember the "Korean chrome" used on automobiles and household appliances during the early 1950s? Do you remember Henry Ford's remarkable foresight to see the ordinary man as his ultimate customer? Ford's innovative marketing strategy of mass production enabled the first Model T to roll off the assembly line on October 1, 1908, and begin America's undying love affair with the automobile.

Since then, songs have been sung about automobiles. Jokes have been made; books have been written; people have been born and married, have lived and died in cars. The freedom and pleasure that cars afford are unmeasurable.

Many a young person's first dream is of the car he or she will someday own. That car will be the ultimate vehicle, not just a daily driver. That dream car will be faster than any other, and will attract that special boy or girl. It will be the envy of all. Do we ever grow up? Bumper stickers that I have seen lately suggest not—such as "The Only Difference Between a Man and a Boy is the Price of His Toys," and "He Who Dies with the Most Toys Wins."

What automobile was the subject of your dreams? Was it a Model A or T Ford? A bright red Pierce Arrow? A Chevrolet Camero, Ford Mustang, Studebaker, Hudson or any of the other trendy cars that have come and gone over the past century? If you were not able to own your dream car in your youth, you may find it slumbering on one of these pages. It's never too late.

The love for the new American automobile doesn't seem nearly as strong today compared to past years, but the love of the older auto seems to be as strong as ever. Have you ever watched a sixty- or seventy-year-old person when he or she sees a Model A driving by? Their eyes light up like a child's at Christmas. Someday when I'm out driving my Model A and this happens, I'm going to stop and ask them if they would like a ride just for old time's sake.

People in their sixties and seventies are not the only ones who love these cars. Their children and grandchildren are the ones who search fields, backroads, salvage yards, and want ads for one of these cars to restore or to fix up the way that they feel it should have been built originally.

Most of the cars pictured in this book are for sale. A few are so well hidden that I would not be able to find them again; we discovered them by accident. Some are right along the main highways and some are on the forgotten byways. Each car has its own story to tell as do the people who own them.

Previous page
Mystery shrouds this abandoned mid-thirties Chrysler. Picturesquely covered with lush green foliage in a remote area of northwestern Minnesota, it's a true diamond in the rough. I found it a few yards off the main highway, within the village limits of Erskine, Minnesota. No longer wanted by its owner, this car was parked and forgotten.

In 1947 Ford advertised the slogan, "There's a Ford in Your Future." This Ford from the past could still have a future under a restorer's magic touch. I found it behind a service station on US Highway 2 in northwestern Minnesota. Silent and alone, in a field of wildflowers and weeds, the 1947 Ford Super Deluxe Tudor is a proud survivor. It was a carryover of the 1946 model except for a few minor changes such as elimination of the red stripe on the grille. The parking lights for 1947 were circular and mounted under the headlights, rather than the rectangular lights of the 1946 model. Notice the hood ornament; it was available only on models made late in the year. The emblem on the base of the hood signified whether the car sported a six-cylinder or V-8 engine.

Thousands of car enthusiasts braved 100 degree weather to attend the 1988 annual Back To The 50's weekend car show and swap meet in St Paul, Minnesota. Swap meets generally offer lots of unique old car items. One of the items for sale this day was a popular and attractive 1936 Chevrolet Standard Sedan Delivery, one of 9,404 units produced that year. Completely unrestored, it had an asking price of $650. Notice the bumper and grille in the picture—they do not belong on this sedan. A few noteworthy events took place for Chevrolet in 1936, which helped it regain the number one sales position over Ford. Among them was the introduction of hydraulic brakes, as well as an all-steel Turret Top for standard models.

13

Previous page

A golden evening sun shines on this private collection set against a backdrop of sturdy pines. Their resting place is part of a dairy farm in east-central Minnesota, near the city of St. Cloud. The Studebaker Champion three-passenger Business Coupe Regal Deluxe was one of only 3,379 built in 1947, with an original price of $1,451. The stainless steel windshield trim and stainless steel rocker panel moldings identify it as a Regal Deluxe. New for 1947 were the no-glare aircraft dials on the instrument panel and self-adjusting brakes. This Studebaker wears two popular add-on accessories of the fifties: a spotlight and bumper guards.

Tall green grass nestles this rare Chrysler 300F, located in the Indianhead country of western Wisconsin. All Chrysler cars were completely restyled for the 1960 model, and featured unibody construction. This 300F came equipped with a 413 ci V-8 engine, rating 375 horsepower at 5000 rpm in the standard model with an optional version, the 400 horsepower, at 5200 rpm. All the standard features of a New Yorker, plus power swivel seats, were included in the 300F. The 964 300Fs were built in Detroit, each at the factory price of $5,411. Note the trunk decklid with its simulated spare tire outline, a standard on all 300F models. The 1960 300Fs were noted for their speed and power, even winning the first six places in the Flying Mile runs at Daytona, where the winner averaged nearly 145 mph. At Bonneville that same year the 300F won with an average speed of 172.6 mph. Through the grapevine I heard that this car is not for sale, but as they say, everything has its price!

16

The evening sun permeates this isolated 1939 LaSalle four-door near Milaca, Minnesota. It is part of a large private collection that rests in a farm field, among brown grass and pines. Note that the beautiful LaSalle grille is missing. A lot of these grilles were salvaged by customizers in the 1950s, the trick thing to do being to fit them neatly into the front of a 1936 Ford. The LaSalle was extensively restyled for 1939, adding a substantial glass area. The four-door Touring Sedan was the most popular 1939 LaSalle. All LaSalles that year were powered by a 322 ci, 125 horsepower, V-8 engine. A sliding Sunshine Roof was an option available on two-door and four-door sedans. At first glance the bullet-shaped headlamps appear to be missing, but look closely—they are still there.

This 1947 Ford Super Deluxe sedan coupe was rescued from a former used car lot in northern Minnesota by Ken Bird. Bird manages a concrete supply company, but his hobby is buying and selling restorable used cars, especially Fords. The used car lot owner habitually gleaned his less desirable trade-ins and drove them into a field behind his business. During a 40 year period about 125 cars ended up there. Most of them had been stripped, but a lot of them were like this Ford—virtually rust-free. This car is currently undergoing restoration. Unfortunately, the rest of the cars were not rescued in time, and were crushed before Bird had the time and money to take them home. The owner of the used car lot, an elderly man, said the crusher paid him more money then he had ever earned in parting them out over the last few years. A lot of really good cars were lost, all a matter of economics.

I first found this 1950 Mercury in Dawson, Minnesota, as part of a private collection owned by a Ford enthusiast. The owner, who does not advertise for privacy's sake, is a friendly person and knowledgeable about cars, especially which ones are worth saving and how to restore them. While I was in his yard, I thought to myself what a classy cruiser this car would make. Later I learned that the car has a new home in Sioux City, Iowa, waiting to be made into a Lead Sled. Mercury's best year was 1950. That was the year Mercury was chosen to be the Indianapolis 500 pace car. The one-millionth Mercury produced was a 1950 four-door sedan. Only minor trim changes differentiated it from the 1949 models. The base price of a 1950 Mercury two-door coupe was $1,875 and 151,489 of them were produced. Optional equipment included Touch-O-Matic transmission with overdrive, oil bath air cleaner, heater, two-tone paint, whitewall tires, radio, and power seats.

Located in southwestern Minnesota, and part of a private collection of cars and parts assembled over the years, is this 1935 Chrysler Airflow. It rests among wagonloads of miscellaneous bodies and parts. The most popular Chrysler Airflow for 1935 was the six-passenger sedan using a 115 horsepower engine. It originally cost $2,245. Restoration would be considerable work, but the end result would be worthy of envy. Only 69 Chrysler Airflow Custom Imperial C-3s were originally built.

23

Previous page
When you take an evening drive down a tranquil country road you never know where treasures wait. The drive is even more enjoyable when you know that at the end of the journey you will find a pot of gold. It happened to us one night when a fellow tin hunter escorted us to the farm that houses this private collection of cars near Milaca, Minnesota. The owner of the farm is quite a collector. What year is this car? At first glance you can tell something is amiss. It is a 1940 Mercury four-door sedan wearing a 1939 hood. This was only the second year of production for Mercury. Improvements over the 1939 model included sealed-beam headlamps, a two-spoke steering wheel, a steering column-mounted gearshift, and vent wing windows. The most popular car with Mercury buyers was the four-door Town Sedan priced at $987.

When traveling, I like to plan trips so we can explore out-of-the-way small towns. We found this 1954 Mercury Monterey hardtop parked and abandoned in a declining village in west-central Minnesota right off US Highway 59. If you drive through this town, look closely because it's not the only old collectible car there. The most notable changes for 1954 were the wraparound vertical taillights and the restyled grille. Chrome rocker panels and fender skirts were standard equipment. A unique counterpart to this Mercury Monterey hardtop was the Sun Valley Sport Coupe, which was basically the same car except it had a plexiglas insert in the roof. The factory price for the Monterey Hardtop was $2,452. An additional $130 bought you the Sun Valley option.

A pair of ever-popular 1930 Model As, a Fordor sedan and a coupe, sit in a field in northern Minnesota, just waiting to be resurrected back to their glory days. As we entered the city of Crookston, Minnesota, we saw the signs for the Polk County Museum, and decided to see what this one had to offer. We hadn't yet stopped the car before we spotted these two ladies. Needless to say, the museum came in second on our priority list. After examining the cars, we toured the museum and discovered that it had a display of early cars that is worth checking out, plus lots of other interesting antiques. Henry Ford saw the ordinary man on the street as his ultimate customer, rather than the wealthy. On October 20, 1927, he introduced the Model A to a huge market. It was such a success that nearly 400,000 people put a down payment on one within two weeks of its introduction. In 1930 Ford sold 1,155,162 Model As, produced in nine different models.

Swap meets are another good place to find project cars. This 1939 Buick four-door sedan was brought to a Chippewa Falls, Wisconsin, swap meet to be sold. The Midwest is becoming more active each year in the old car hobby. A few years ago swap meets and car shows occurred occasionally, but now you can attend at least one event or sometimes two or three events on any weekend from April through October.

Richly forested northern Minnesota is worth exploring for older tin. Hidden by nature was a 1957 Dodge two-door Royal Lancer hardtop, one of the few cars that did not meet the crusher when this area was cleared out. The 1955 Ford sitting beside it was not as lucky. The 1957 was one of Dodge's most memorable years, with its new finned rear fenders and Torsion-Aire ride replacing the coil springs of previous years. More than 95 percent of all 1957 Dodges had automatic transmissions. This forested area is now more solitary without all of its four-wheeled inhabitants.

32

I couldn't resist snapping another picture of a Model A Ford. What is it about these cars that people love? This rural setting is another of the small towns I visited in South Dakota. The weathered Quonset hut appears to be nearly the age of the car, which makes me wonder what is behind the closed doors. There was no one in sight the day I stopped to inquire, but there were a few other cars hiding on the other side of the building.

This special edition 1950 Ford Crestliner is highly prized by collectors today for its rarity and unusual looks. This vehicle is sitting in a row with other collector cars on the edge of a cornfield. The vehicles are owned by Todd Buer, an avid Ford collector. In an effort to boost sales, Ford introduced the 1950 Crestliner as a late-season offering. It was basically a Custom Tudor Sedan with special trim. Standard equipment included a vinyl roof, special side trim, gold Crestliner nameplate, full wheel covers, two-tone paint, and a lavish color-keyed interior. They came with a V-8 engine only. Selling for $1,711 and weighing 3,050 pounds, 17,601 Crestline units were produced in 1950.

34

Salvage yards—not junkyards!

I quickly received an education on what to call a yard full of cars. To call it a junkyard is a put-down to the owner. I was corrected more than once for a slip of the tongue, so if you want to walk into a yard full of old cars and parts, remember that you are going into a salvage yard, not a junkyard. The pieces are not junk but valuable inventory. Shown here is only a small sampling of what is really out there to find. The tin is not all gone, the search has just become more challenging.

What is it about salvage yards that draws people to spend days browsing through them? Why would anyone plan their vacation route by the location of salvage yards? I've done just that for years, and I'm not sure if I can answer these questions. I believe that I came upon my love of cars by osmosis. The x-marks on our maps note the treasures of old cars and salvage yards. Over the past few years we have traveled many miles looking for old tin; some trips were profitable, some were not.

We heard of one group of cars in northern Minnesota—some real beauties, it was rumored—so we decided to see what was there. So as not to trespass we stopped at a gas station to get directions. The gas station was closed, out to lunch, so we drove around town, had something to eat, and came back. The station was open now. We found that the station was once a used car dealership that harbored trade-ins. The cars were driven out in the lot, parked, and never resold. What a find!

It was sheer luck that brought us to this yard the day we arrived. We were able to capture the cars on film, but it was too late to salvage them; they had been sold for the price of the metal. The crusher came in a day later and now they are gone. In 1988 the price of metal was at an all time high and a drought caused marshy areas, where abandoned cars are stored, to dry making them accessible. Many yards were cleaned out; their gems crushed, making the remaining cars even more valuable.

Salvage yard owners are as varied as the cars that they collect. Some thought we were a little strange when we asked to take pictures. Most owners were friendly and would bend over backward to accommodate us. One didn't trust us and sent his nine-year-old daughter along to make sure we didn't steal anything.

A lot of people would be envious of this young lady; she knew every make and model they had and where they were located. Her dad even had a car set aside for each of his kids, and most of them were 1955, 1956, or 1957 Chevrolets.

Previous page
A 1955 Chrysler New Yorker Deluxe Series St. Regis sits in a salvage yard in Grand Forks, North Dakota, but it appears well-preserved. Chrysler introduced free-standing taillights in 1955 on the upper edges of each rear fender. The two-tone styling on this car was unique to the St. Regis. The factory price of $3,690 did not include options such as white sidewall tires, chrome wire wheels, Air Temp air-conditioning, Solex glass, fog lights, and windshield washers.

A 1939 Willys Overland Model manufactured in Toledo, Ohio, was offered only one year in this body style. Grand Forks, North Dakota, is the present home of this unique two-door sedan. Removing a few dents, repairing the surface rust and replacing the windows would transform this car into a neat cruiser. The Overland had a 102 inch wheelbase, four-cylinder engine, new hydraulic brakes, and a base price of $689. In 1939 Willys Overland offered two lines of cars—the Overland and the Willys—and a total of 16 models. The Overland had a compression ratio of 6.35:1, while the Willys, a 5.70:1. Both models were equipped with eight-gallon fuel tanks.

Mother Nature, if undisturbed, can create beauty in the strangest places. Discovering this car and recording it in this picture made all the unsuccessful journeys worthwhile. Removing this 1947 Chevrolet four-door from this place of rest would not be an easy task. It may be best to let it remain as it is. The license plate shows that the last time this car was registered was in 1960. Therefore I would guess the tree to be at least 25 years old.

To remove the car, you would have to unbolt the front clip or saw down the tree. The tree must have known that to grow in a rare car would shorten its life, so it picked a more common four-door. I wonder what happened to the ever-dependable Stovebolt Six engine? Do you suppose that the engine was blown up and it proved too large a job to repair? If you want this car or more information, journey to Kaylor, South Dakota.

Resting on its top in Park River, North Dakota, is a 1948 Chevrolet. It seems that it may have been overturned because someone wanted to salvage parts from the undercarriage. Little is left of this car, except for the bumper, brake drums and springs, none of which are rare. The last year Chevrolet used the 1942 prewar styling was 1948, with only slight modifications to the grille. This Chevrolet Fleetline Aero Sedan was the production leader for 1948, one of 211,861 cars selling for $1,434 each. A common complaint of car owners was the horizontal rear window, which caused poor rear visibility.

A gentle rolling hillside often frequented by whitetail deer, rabbits, and other wildlife is the resting place for a 1957 Chevrolet and several other relics from days gone by. "The Sweet, Smooth, and Sassy," the 1957 Chevrolet. Originally, this car sold for $2,274. At today's market value, the car completely restored would sell for nearly $8,000. In the car's present condition, with restorable front fenders and hood, it can be purchased for a few hundred dollars. Chevrolet lost its first place sales spot to Ford in 1957, partly because America did not buy the car with the enthusiasm Chevrolet had anticipated. Today the much-loved 1957 Chevy has a different impact on the American public. The most popular style for 1957 was the Series 210 four-door sedan. This picture features one of the 260, 401 cars produced in that series. Chevrolet claimed that the new 283 ci V-8 engine was the first automobile engine to provide one horsepower per cubic inch.

Previous page

Jim's Auto Salvage in Hutchinson, Minnesota, is the current home of approximately 1,000 automobiles from the 1940s to the mid-seventies. One of Jim's cars is this 1960 Ford, with the tree growing in the engine compartment. The car is pretty well intact, except that the engine and hood have been removed. I would estimate from the size of the tree that this car has been parked in its present location for at least 15 years. To salvage this neat machine, some effort would be involved but the end result would be worth it. Ford completely restyled in 1960. Many people liked this new style, but many more didn't. In the Galaxie Special Series was a hardtop, the Special Starliner, priced at $2,275. The sleek styling was not only good looking, it also improved the aerodynamics for places like Daytona. At 213.7 inches long and 81.5 inches wide, the 1960 Ford was the longest, lowest, and widest car ever made by the Ford division of Ford Motor Company. The width made it illegal for highway operation in most states if driven without proper marker lights. Edsels, Mercurys, Chevrolets, and Oldsmobiles were also too wide to be legal. Law enforcement agencies agreed to look the other way if manufacturers would correct the problem on future models.

A faded red 1966 Plymouth Barracuda has to share its pasture with children, cows, horses, thistles, a few trees, and other cars. I found this inviting salvage yard driving down a primary road near Detroit Lakes, Minnesota. The day was beautiful, the scenery was picturesque, the company was stimulating. What more could anyone ask for? The 1966 Barracuda was the first year this model sported a Barracuda fish emblem. The base price for a V-8 model, at $2,637, included standard rocker panel moldings, carpets, special full wheel covers, and bucket seats. Vinyl tops were an option.

46

Studebakers manufactured in South Bend, Indiana, took the thirteenth position in car manufacturing in 1937. This Studebaker President Eight Custom Sedan was one of 80,993 cars produced. Accessory bumper guards were an option for 1937; the pair on this car are still in restorable condition. Do you need a pair? They can be located in one of four yards in Grand Forks, North Dakota. Between the yards there are more than 7,000 cars—so say the advertisements—but I didn't count them. To open the alligator hood on this car, you had to twist the hood ornament. I've never owned a Studebaker, but it seems that with little effort this car could be retrieved and restored.

48

The ads for Porter Auto Repair & Salvage in Park River, North Dakota, claim that approximately 2,000 vehicles are supposed to be in the yard, and that they had been in business for more than 20 years, making it just the type of yard I like to browse through. Times had changed, poor economy and the drought of 1988 hit this area hard. The body shop has been closed down and many of the cars have been crushed and sold for the price of the metal. As you can see, the yard looks almost bare. A few of the more desirable cars and all the trucks were salvaged. Why this Chevrolet was saved is anyone's guess; there doesn't appear to be much left on it to salvage. During the early fifties, the sporty Bel Air was a welcome addition to the Chevy line. Only a few changes were made in 1954, such as the addition of more teeth in the grille. The six-passenger four-door sedan, like the pictured car, was the most popular model, selling 248,750 at a list price of $1,884. Identifying the Bel Air are the full length sweepspear molding and rear fender double molding. The 1954 model was the end of this body style before the dramatic changes of 1955; this was also the last year of the Woodie. From this year on all Woodies would be made by special order only.

This 1958 Ford Custom Series four-door appears to be a member of the Pepsi generation. The 1958 Ford front end and rear end were completely restyled but were still interchangeable with the 1957. The public didn't agree with Ford's new styling, because 1958 car sales slumped and allowed Chevrolet to return to the number one position after being in second place to Ford in 1957. The new changes included a simulated air scoop on the hood, a honeycomb grille, and dual headlamps on each front fender. Cruise-O-matic transmissions were offered. A new type of air suspension, used only in 1958, consisted of plastic balloons placed within the coil springs, not a good idea.

A lone sentinel, resting among the pines in northern Wisconsin, is one of the 779 Chrysler Royal Six six-passenger coupes made in early 1942 before World War II. Note the chrome: later models had trim in matching colors because all chrome went to support the war effort. The stainless steel moldings have survived the years of weathering better than the body. There is surface rust on the car, but otherwise it has fared well. The brake light on the trunk lid was fairly common on cars of the forties and fifties, especially Chryslers—who says collision avoidance lights are a new idea?

53

Previous page

A Pontiac station wagon may not be the dream car of many restorers, but to me this wagon is rather unique, or do I just have a love for the unusual? I owned two station wagons in the past and loved them both. A 1955 Pontiac station wagon Chieftain 870 like this one sold new for $2,603. This was the year, to no one's surprise, that Pontiac followed the rest of the carmakers to introduce the V-8 engine. Pontiac not only had a new engine, but also a totally new body style for 1955. Silver Streaks, the bands on the car hood, are still eye catching today. Common complaints of Chieftain 870 station wagon owners were leaking tailgates and leaking shock absorbers.

Want something other than a Ford or Chevrolet to restore? This 1940 Nash Ambassador is a rare find. I discovered it in a Grand Forks, North Dakota, yard. There may be lots of surface rust, but the body is fairly good overall. It could be a long search before you found another grille, and this one is in sad shape. The Weather Eye heating system was still offered by Nash in 1940. The sedan models came with either a fastback trunk or a humpback trunk at no additional cost. Air foam seating was also standard. Nash offered three lines and 18 models in 1940, each with a 20 gallon gas tank. The base price for a coupe was $1,170.

Sheep and Barracudas seem to get along . . . at least in this salvage yard. The most popular Plymouth for 1965 was the Barracuda, a sporty compact; it was the first year that Valiant was dropped from the Barracuda name. Bucket seats were standard equipment in all Barracudas, as were three-speed manual transmissions, but optional transmissions were the Torqueflite automatic and the four-speed manual floor shift. Normally you hear of a junkyard dog, but this South Dakota salvage yard was the first that I had seen that kept junkyard sheep. Since they kept the grass continually mowed, it was truly a delight walking in this yard. No bugs, snakes, weeds, or brush . . . only neat collections of cars, trucks, and other oddities dragged in over time.

You can see more than cows out to pasture in this western Minnesota yard. Resting here are a pair of 1935 Ford Tudor sedans, some old snowmobiles, and much more. Ford outsold Chevrolet in 1935, the only year in the thirties that they managed to do this. It may have been due in part to Ford's all-new body. This was the last year for Ford's famous welded spoke wheel before it was redesigned, making it one inch smaller and wider to reduce tire roll around corners. The standard brakes were still mechanical, but Ford offered a new, more powerful design. The 1935 frame was much improved over the 1934 because of its double channel construction. The spring suspension was also vastly improved on the passenger cars: the front springs were made much longer and were moved four inches in front of the axle. Options offered on the 1935 were a vanity mirror, selling for an additional 60 cents, side-mirrors, and a defroster. The color choices for 1935 were medium luster black, cordoba gray, and vineyard green. On June 2, 1935, the two-millionth V-8 rolled off the Ford assembly line.

The 1967 model was the second year of production for the ever-popular Dodge Charger. The only changes from the 1966 models were the new grille and fender-top chrome strips with turn signal indicators. For all you Dodge fans, this one is part of a car collection within Weekly's Auto Parts of Grand Forks, North Dakota.

Ragged ragtops

America has always had a love for the open road, a love that naturally extended to open cars. Convertibles were popular when they were first introduced and are still coveted today.

Maybe their allure was due to the fact that the top folded back, allowing a feeling of total driving freedom, the wind blowing in your hair. Maybe they were sought out as a collectors item because at one time, in later years, the convertible was not manufactured as a mass-production car. Whatever the reason, the convertible was generally the most expensive car offered in any model line; this value remains today. Pick up a current old car value guide and, if you check prices, you will find that the convertible holds its value reasonably well.

In our travels we were unable to locate many convertibles in the rough, but in checking car shows and garages, we found many that have been revived and restored.

Previous page

With its top in tatters, this 1952 Packard 250 convertible stands in a ghostly manner, reminiscent of the glory days when it was a more prestigious car. Packard was completely redesigned for 1951, and the 1952 models kept the design except for minor trim changes. Mechanically the cars were also unchanged, except for new optional Easamatic power brakes. The Packard 250 Series featured a 327 ci inline L-head eight-cylinder engine rated at 150 hp. The convertible had a luxurious interior of top grain leather and woven leather-like plastic. And fitting its image, the base price for this car was $3,476.

Mother Nature left little cover on this trio of ragtops: a 1951 Ford, a 1954 Ford, and a 1949 Dodge Coronet convertible coupe. The cloth top is the first part of any convertible to be rotted by sun and moisture. When the top starts to leak, the seats and carpet get wet; this in turn starts the process of interior destruction, until even the floorboards rot out. The 1951 Ford's destruction process accelerated because it was also burnt. There were 2,411 Dodge Coronet coupes produced in 1949, of which this is one of the few remaining. In 1951 Ford offered the new Fordomatic transmission on both the six and V-8 engines. In 1954 the Ford flathead engine was replaced with the new overhead valve V-8. Also new for 1954 were power steering and brakes.

Everyone knows the rumors about junkyard dogs. Usually, they are trained to eat you alive if you so much as breathe on their cars. Yet this dog—as well as many others we encountered—was very friendly. The car he's guarding is a 1951 Lincoln Cosmopolitan convertible. Once upon a time, the prestige and luxury of this Lincoln was the envy of many; today it slumbers under a sky of cotton-like clouds and beautiful sunshine. The Lincoln Cosmopolitan convertible was Lincoln Mercury's most expensive and heaviest model in 1951; this was the final season it was produced. Some of the convenience options were a heater, power windows, radio, and whitewall tires— remember the wide whitewalls? Standard equipment included stainless steel rocker moldings and fender skirts (missing on this car). New features offered in 1951 were a new grille, emblems, vertical taillights, wheelcovers, bumpers, and the Hydra-matic transmission. Sales for Lincoln Mercury in 1951 flourished because people who still had the Korean War fresh in their minds bought a new car whether they needed it or not. They didn't want to go without again.

Grand Forks, North Dakota, is the home of this diamond sandwiched between rows of other derelict cars. An Impala convertible, Chevrolet's heaviest and most expensive car for 1961, it sold for $2,954. Triple taillights, wide side moldings with contrasting insert panels, and a crossed checkered flags emblem centered on the deck lid and rear fender easily identify this car as an Impala. Standard equipment on the 64,600 units produced included a parking brake, backup light, glove compartment, dual sun visors, electric windshield wipers, cigar lighter, and deluxe steering wheel. All V-8s had oil filters and oil-bath-type air cleaners. Some of the options were a Positraction rear axle, tinted glass, padded instrument panel, heavy-duty battery, dual exhausts, air conditioning, windshield washers, radio, and four-way power seats. This Chevy may need a few parts to restore, but it would be fun to tool around in when finished.

A 1965 Mustang convertible—a milestone car—is one of many cars owned by a Ford enthusiast in southern Minnesota. Each of his children get to pick their favorite Mustang from his stock, help restore it, and then it's theirs. His gift to me was allowing me to spend a beautiful May afternoon strolling through his private collection and the time he took out of his busy day to share his love of cars with me. People like these make the world a better place to live in. The Mustang is as popular with collectors today as it was with new car buyers in 1965. More than half a million were sold from its introduction in mid-1964 to year-end 1965. The 1965 models, very similar to the 1964½ models, contained an alternator in place of a generator. Some of the standard equipment for 1965 included heater, defroster, dual sun visors, seatbelts, vinyl upholstery, and black sidewall tires. This survivor is one of 73,112 Mustang convertibles produced at a list price of $2,614 each.

Tired workhorses

Shortly after the car was invented, it became evident that something with more load space and power was desired. Something to do the heavy work, the heavy hauling, necessitated inventing the truck, the metal workhorse.

Depending on the job that needed to be done, workhorses came in many variations. The tired workhorses pictured here are just a few. The larger one-and-one-half-ton truck, the Model TT, the pickup, and the sedan delivery. In the seventies and eighties, the workhorse trucks were no longer just utility vehicles. They have become more luxurious, and are often used as family vehicles as well.

These tired workhorses are now out to pasture, awaiting the arrival of someone ready to revive them after their much-deserved rest.

The declining community of Niagara, North Dakota, is home to a retired and abandoned 1938 Chevrolet one-and-one-half-ton truck positioned next to an old weathered blacksmith shop. Niagara is not a ghost town, but one of the few remaining towns I've discovered that has a dirt main street. In 1937 the Chevrolet truck line received all-new sheet metal conforming to the styling of the new cars. For 1938 there were few styling changes other than on the hood panels and grilles. When these trucks were doing heavy hauling, the hood side panels could be removed for extra cooling.

Previous page

A handsome pair of Ford pickups, spotted near Hutchinson, Minnesota. The pickup in the foreground sports a Port-a-wall, the fake whitewall tire on the front. The Port-a-wall, an option available in the late fifties, was positioned between the tire and the wheel rim before the tire was aired up, so that the inflation of the tire held the Port-a-wall in place. Sometimes it took several tries before it was positioned correctly. The Ford pickup was completely restyled for 1938: an all-new cab, front-end sheet metal, rear fenders, pickup body, and running boards. Ford finally adopted hydraulic brakes in 1939; they also greatly improved the 85 hp V-8 engine and made dual downdraft carburetors the standard equipment on all V-8 engines. The significant differences in the 1939 pickup over the 1938 model include a lower hood ornament, latch handle and standard passenger car hubcaps. The V-8 emblem on the center of the grille was deleted along with the standard rear bumper. Can you distingish the 1938 model from the 1939?

A Ford Model TT Closed Cab truck is spotted among changing fall colors in this western Wisconsin field. Shortly after I was told of its whereabouts, it was sold—another tired workhorse that has come out of retirement to afford pleasure to a new owner. The Ford Closed Cab for the TT was introduced in April 1925 and featured plate-glass door windows (which could be raised or lowered by means of a strap!), an adjustable windshield, rubber floor mats, and dispatch boxes. A new option for 1925 was a hand-operated windshield wiper. The bare chassis was priced at $365; the closed cab option was priced at $85, and the open cab at $65.

76

This US Mail collection truck, originally from North Dakota, is not in as good a condition as it looks. Notice the rust holes on the left side. It appears to have lain on its side in the dirt for years. The rear door was mint; it had been sold for $800. Other than new old stock, it would have been difficult to find one as cherry. Ford's significant styling changes in 1938 are evident on this sedan delivery: new front fenders, grille, hood, hood sides, and hub caps. With this new look and features, it still fell in the $700 price range. I wish I could find a restored one for that price today.

Telltale features

In the automobile's early days, features such as headlights, taillights, engines, tail fins, and moldings uniquely identified one model, make, or year. If you did not grow up during this era, it may seem impossible to identify a car by these features, but it really is not that difficult. To tell one car part from another is like learning anything else—take it one part at a time. The archaeology of this hobby is only one of its many fascinating aspects.

The minute information contained in this chapter is not meant to fully educate you in the distinguishable features of cars. The items I have included here are what I felt were different, unusual, and intact.

The sun is shining, the thistles are in colorful bloom, and I have discovered another unusual jewel. The taillight of a 1956 Chrysler Windsor seems to be a natural extension of the rear bumper ends. Intact after all these years, it still attracts the camera for its neat looks and styling.

Oldsmobile restyled its taillights for 1957 and, after 32 years, the pair is still attractive with its chrome triangle molding in the center, chromed brow, and oval shape. Another unique and popular feature of the 1957 Oldsmobile was the pillared rear window, partially shown here.

An unusual 1961 Dodge Seneca station
wagon taillight with the same style of
taillight as on the 1961 Dodge Polara.
When I first spotted the taillight I thought
it appeared almost futuristic. I wonder if
any customizers have molded it into
another body style?

The suns rays gleam off a 1958 Chevrolet taillight—one of three different taillights that Chevrolet offered for 1958. The Impala had three separate round lights, the station wagon had one round light, and all the other models used this double lens arrangement in a single housing. The 1958 Chevrolet was a brand new car from the ground, up. A new suspension system of inflated air bags was available for the first time: the Air Ride. For an additional $32 you could get the two-tone paint option this car so proudly wears. The 1958 Chevy had a 117.5 inch wheelbase. All models were 209 inches long, thus making the 1958 much bigger than previous cars. The standard V-8 engine was the ever popular 283 ci, first introduced in 1957. Many people in their thirties have a soft spot in their heart for this car; it is often the first new car they remember riding in. Memories of past experiences seem to make certain models more desirable.

84

This grille may have been designed to fit the 1955 DeSoto, but it is popular today among designers of Lead Sleds and Customs. The day we took this picture, the car was precariously close to the jaws of the crusher. The Erskine, Minnesota, used car dealership was due to be cleaned up and crushed the day I arrived. I made an offer for the grille and after some discussion, was able to purchase, disassemble and save it. Now I will have to get an early 1950s car to fit it into. One of the teeth is a bit tarnished, so I will need to find a replacement or rechrome the grille. Note the pancake hood—it came stock on this DeSoto. In the 1950s, customizers would spend hundreds of hours trying to bend and shape other car hoods so that they achieved the pancake appearance. It's just too bad that this car was a four-door sedan or I may have tried to purchase yet another car.

87

A 1940 Chevrolet carries the remains of a tree cut down in its prime to avoid the destruction of the bumper. I spotted this car and several others parked off Highway 14 in southwestern Minnesota, next to an old gas station of the same vintage. These cars are not too far from the banks of Plum Creek of Laura Ingalls Wilder fame. In 1940 the 25 millionth Chevrolet rolled out of the factory, a Master Deluxe two-door town sedan.

How far the engine has evolved to advance from this to the speed and reliability of the modern engine! The Hurricane, a six-cylinder Willys engine, produced 90 hp and had a bore and stroke of 3⅛ x 3½ inches for a piston displacement of 161 ci. The compression ratio was 7.6:1. The three-speed transmission with an optional overdrive made 35 mpg possible.

Problems haunted the Ford Flathead V-8 since production began in March of 1932, primarily because the engine was not completely tested before put into production. Modifying the pistons and distributor and adding a duplex Stromberg carburetor improved the V-8. All the Ford Flathead V-8 engines were produced at the Ford Rouge plant and shipped to other plants for installation. The Ford V-8s were of the L-head design with 90 degree crankshaft configuration, and from 1932 through 1941, were

painted Ford engine green. They grew from 221 ci displacement in 1932 to 239 ci in 1953. The compression ratio in 1932 was 5.5:1; in 1953 it was 7.2:1. Holley carburetors were used in the 1953 model. Henry Ford took quite a gamble on the V-8 engine. If it had not worked out, it could have been the end of the Ford Motor Company. But the gamble paid off. During the first two days after the V-8 was introduced, nearly six million people came out to view Ford's latest success.

Our world, full of variety and surprises, never ceases to amaze me. As I neared this Mercury, I startled away a bird that flew to a nearby tree and perched there, scolding me. Curiosity sent me searching and I quickly discovered that the Mercury heater box was being used as an incubator. What ingenuity on the part of this mother bird! Mother Nature shares many secrets with us if we take the time to discover what she has to say. I quickly captured this picture and then left the mother bird to return to her nurturing duties.

91

Mascots or hood ornaments—a true telltale feature. It's not known when the first car mascot was made. They had no mechanical reason to be there, but they had the vital role of adding a personal touch to one's car. Mascots were nearly all custom-made in the early years of motoring. By the late twenties mascots were so popular that automobile manufacturers decided to provide their own mascots either as standard equipment or as an accessory. In the mid-thirties Packard produced two price ranges of automobiles: on the expensive models, a pelican hood ornament was perched; on the less-expensive models stood the Goddess of Speed mascot, also known as the doughnut pusher. This mascot became the longest lived mascot in United States automobile history. Although it underwent many changes, it was used from 1926 until 1950.

The kiss of rust

The Midwestern states of America accommodate many weather extremes. Temperatures can be as high as 106 degrees Fahrenheit and as low as 40 degrees below. We experience rain, hail, sleet, high humidity, tornados, frost, and whatever else Mother Nature decides we need—sometimes several extremes mixed within a twenty-four-hour period.

The combination of these elements is destructive to many things, but is especially dangerous to exposed manmade material. Tin has faired better in other parts of the country, but don't let that discourage your search for tin in the Midwest, some have survived the elements remarkably.

Rust is the blight that forms when air and moisture meet exposed iron or steel. This DeSoto brake drum, a victim of neglect, has more than its share of rust. I wonder why the fender is still intact and the brake drum so deteriorated?

Weathering, moisture, humidity, and dirt are a curse to cars. This Ford Mainline must have spent many of its later years lying on its side to be so badly deteriorated. Rust only slowly destroys, compared to the crusher. This picture shows another of the many cars that were crushed in the northern Minnesota yard cleaned out in the summer of 1988. The Crestline, Mainline, and Customline were the three great new lines of cars offered by Ford in 1952. There were 11 body styles and 18 models. The Korean War created a shortage of chrome, so all 1952 cars were equipped with an inferior product later known as Korean chrome. The 1952 Ford line was completely restyled. This restyling plus material shortages delayed the introduction of this model, making its debut on February 1, 1952. Mainline models were the least expensive of the three new lines, offering a horn button in place of a horn ring. The sun visor and armrest were on the driver's side only.

96

Forgotten and weathered by time,
laminated safety glass does not withstand
the test when moisture penetrates between
the layers.

An R series International pickup, succumbed to old age, sits in a dense thicket near Hayward, Wisconsin, just growing moss. The biggest change for the R series truck was the open grille with the single bar between the headlights. International trucks—both the L and the R series—had a hood that opened from either side or could be fully removed if both latches were released. Automatic transmissions and power steering were options. International had a history of building rugged trucks for dependable service and the R series upheld that tradition.

After nearly 60 years, little remains of a worn and weathered 1930 Model A interior. The cars are parked within the town limits of Crookston, Minnesota. Time and the elements eventually destroy most manmade items, but when a car interior is left outside as this one has been, the process is quickened.

This 1938 Ford Deluxe four-door has traveled many thousands of miles, by the looks of its interior. In 1938 Ford offered worsted broadcloth interiors in the standard model, and mohair was available at extra cost. Better quality broadcloth and mohair were available on the deluxe models. A very rare, unadvertised option for coupes and sedans was a leatherette or genuine leather interior, available for a few dollars more.

The unique interior of this 1960 Chrysler 300F is still in excellent condition after nearly thirty years. Standard equipment on a 300F consisted of four bucket seats, of which the front ones were dual swivel buckets.

In its prime this 1939 Ford Deluxe
instrument panel had a golden grain
mahogany finish and "modern" gauges
separated by a rustless steel strap. The
Deluxe Fords had a glove compartment
with a clock and a lock. The dash featured
a cigar lighter, ashtray, grille for radio
speaker installation, headlight beam
indicators, choke, throttle, and other
controls. All knobs are recessed into the
panel for safety. Deluxe cars were
equipped with dual wipers, dual sun
visors, and the Deluxe Banjo steering
wheel.

A 1958 Edsel instrument panel and Teletouch-equipped steering column was offered for sale at the Iola, Wisconsin, car show and swap meet in July 1988. It was equipped with safety padded cowling, floating drum-type speedometer, and four circular operating gauge control pods. Edsels were produced by the Ford Motor Company during the 1958, 1959, and 1960 model years.

A goldmine of components

Most hobbyists collect something such as coins, stamps, pictures, or the like. While gathering the pictures for this book I received an education in what other people collect, especially people who love cars.

Pictured on the following pages are collections of crushed cars, wheels, tires, radiators, doors, and road signs. Other collections I have seen are of hub caps, taillights, headlights, hoods, grilles, bumpers, engines, and just about any other car part imaginable. If the room is available, some people simply collect cars.

Another of the many yards we had heard about, that was supposed to contain several jewels, has been cleaned out. The glory days for these five cars are over; the crusher beat you to them. In 1988 the high price of metal combined with a drought caused the demise of many collectible cars in the Midwest.

107

Beauty is in the eye of the beholder, so even a collection of wheels can be beautiful in the right setting. How many million miles do you suppose these wheels have rolled before being laid to rest in this automotive boneyard?

A pile of tires that have traveled their last miles. Where have they traveled to, what have they experienced, and why would anyone collect them?

This part of Minnesota is located in the Corn Belt of the United States, but there must have been a drought or a poor corn crop this year. Why else would you find a corn crib full of radiators, and what would you ever do with them?

Row upon row of doors floating on a sea
of grass. Which one do you need? I'm
sure it must be there.

Stop, Go, Yield, Pavement Ends. You'd better not try to follow these signs or the outcome of your journey will be in doubt.

Diamond clusters

The longer you are involved in collecting, the more cars that you collect. It seems that one is never enough. When you get one car nearly restored, you start thinking of the next project you want to begin. My husband and I have ten cars on our small parcel of land, ranging in age from 1931 to 1967, and I know that our collection is not complete. These do not include our daily drivers, of which the newest one is a 1978.

From traveling around the county and talking to other enthusiasts, I know that we are not alone. Some people have a one-track mind and collect only one make or model; others, more diverse, collect several.

Whether you are a collector of one make or model or whether you love them all, I hope that one of the following photos portrays the car of your dreams.

Abandoned and neglected, a quartet of early 1930s sedans out to pasture after serving their owners well.

Previous page
What a pretty picture! Rows of collectible cars lined up and categorized. Strolling unsupervised through this yard was better than a day at an amusement park. If you get bored with the cars, there are rows of pickups. And if farm machinery is your bag, that's there, too. What part or body are you interested in? Ask yard owner Ziegler King. He knows his inventory.

Ford's slogan for 1956 was, "The Fine Car at Half the Fine Car Price." This 1956 Ford Fairlane Victoria was introduced with a new 12 volt ignition system, ending the previous year car's starting problems. Also new was the electrical system; from this year forward the cars have had a 12 volt system. For 1956, Ford offered Lifeguard safety features: optional padded dashboard covers, improved door locks, optional seatbelts, double-swiveled rearview mirrors, sun visors, and a Deep Dish steering wheel. Maybe next summer I will take the trailer with me so I can bring this one home. I dream of cruising around in this gem. Good thing I'm married to an autobody mechanic.

Here are the sheep, but where are the goats—GTOs? Immersed in surroundings of yesterday, these sheep are unaware of the valuable duty they perform by keeping the grass away from these and approximately 2,000 other cars in a South Dakota yard.

120

Previous page
Are you looking for a 1952, 1953, or 1954 Ford? This collection of Fords, intermingled with birch trees, lies concealed from view of the average passerby. Hayward, Wisconsin, is where I located this picturesque scene.

This pair of Chevys rests in a pasture near Mahnomen, Minnesota—a 1963 Impala and a 1964 Impala Super Sport. Impala Super Sports, identifiable by the wide side spear with the Impala signature at the rear, triple taillights, anodized aluminum rear panel, and front fender trim, are as popular today as they were when they were new. When I see this pair I remember the family next door, and the Impala they drove when I was a child.

Take caution when you go into strange
territory on a tin hunt, you never know
what monsters lie in the grass keeping
watch over the cars.

Odds and ends

You may not agree that the following three pictures fit into this book, but their beauty and uniqueness drew me to them.

Never before have I seen a pedal car or bicycle of this vintage in the rough. Most have been collected by someone else and, if seen at all, are for sale at a swap meet or in a show fully restored.

The fenders and headlights appear to be put here by someone with an artistic touch, or they may be an accident from the past.

Even pedal cars can be found in the rough. I would have loved to have taken this one home for restoration, but space was restrictive. I wonder, will this car perish with the seasons or be reclaimed to fulfill a child's dream?

So long . . .

All good things must come to an end; this is true also of the journey we have just been on. Each time I look at the pictures in this book I find myself drifting back into time, joyfully remembering the many trips down the highways and byways of this lovely country, remembering the car shows and swap meets of the past years and looking with anticipation toward the upcoming season, so that I can continue on with my search. I constantly find myself looking and dreaming of the ideal car, the one I would like to purchase and restore.

The cars that now bring me the pleasure of the search were at one time someone else's pride and joy. Someone bought these cars new off the showroom floor; they worked hard to save the money to pay for them. Oh, the pain and pleasure these vehicles must have brought to their owners! Now they are parked, abandoned and forgotten.

Spring is just around the corner, here in the heartland of America, and when the season changes I will be able to continue on my search. I am looking for the *perfect* 1953 Ford Victoria, like the one I once owned. Maybe this year will be the year that I find my car, but even if I do the journey will not be over, because I, just like many of you, have been bitten by the old car hobby. Without it, life would not be as rich or rewarding.

I wish you the best of luck in finding your dream car, but even if you don't, I'm sure you will enjoy the hunt. Happy travels!

In each person's life, there is a stage where pedal cars are too childish and you're not old enough to drive a real car. A bicycle usually will fill the gap and and for a period of our lives they bring as much pleasure and as many experiences as the automobile. This bicycle, discarded after years of faithful service, was overgrown with weeds when we first discovered it. The designs and models of bicycles are as varied as cars. This bicycle now has a new home and will one day be restored back to a ridable condition. The chicken coop in the background is not as lucky; it will soon be removed to allow for a housing development.